find out about wild animals

Written and edited by
Moira Butterfield
and Nicola Wright

Designed by
Chris Leishman

Illustrated by
Rachael O'Neill

Contents

Chrysalis Children's Books

All kinds of animals

Wild animals live all over the world. There are many different kinds.

Elephant

The mammal group includes the largest animals.

Clown fish

Fish live in rivers, seas and oceans.

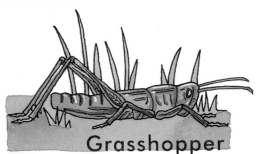

Grasshopper

There are millions of insects.

Snakes are reptiles.

Reptiles live in warm places.

Amphibians can live in water and on land.

Frogs are amphibian.

All birds have wings and feathers.

Flamingo

Animal meals

Some animals only eat plants. They are called **herbivores**.

Zebra

Some animals only eat other animals. They are called **carnivores**.

Leopard

Animals that eat both meat and plants are called **omnivores**.

Out in the cold

At the top and bottom of the Earth there are cold, icy places where only a few different kinds of animals live.

Polar bears can smell seals several kilometres away.

Caribou (also called reindeer) live in big herds.

Fun Fact

Arctic hares and foxes turn white in winter. This helps to hide them on the snow.

Lemmings live in warm underground burrows.

Arctic tern

The far north is called the Arctic. In the middle there is frozen sea. Animals live on the land around the sea.

Antarctic

At the far south of the Earth there is some land called the Antarctic.

Penguins live around Antarctic shores. They cannot fly but they can swim well.

Musk oxen have warm shaggy coats that keep them warm.

Seals have a layer of fat that keeps them warm.

The world's biggest whale, the **blue whale**, swims in the Antarctic Ocean.

Under the sun

Deserts are very dry, hot places. Some of the world's hottest deserts are in North America. Here are a few of the animals found there.

The **roadrunner** bird can run up to 37km/hr.

The **elf owl** is only the size of a sparrow.

The **kangaroo rat** gets water from the seeds it eats.

Spadefoot toads burrow underground to avoid the sun.

The **scorpion** insect has a sting in its tail.

Some desert lizards stand on tiptoe and hold each foot in turn off the ground to stop them burning!

The **rattlesnake** has rattling scales on the end of its tail.

The **Gila monster** is a poisonous lizard.

Camels

Camels can survive for days without food and water. They store it in their humps.

They have wide feet that stop them sinking in the sand.

They can close up their nostrils to keep out sand.

7

Deep in the forest

In northern parts of the world there are huge forests. Lots of different animals live amongst the trees.

Raccoon

Woodpeckers peck tree bark to find tasty insects.

Moose

Porcupines have strong claws for climbing trees. Their sharp quills protect them from attackers.

Brown bear

Owls nest in the trees. They hunt at night.

Squirrel

Beaver

A **lynx** is a type of wild cat.

Busy beavers

Beavers can gnaw through trees. They drag the branches to a stream to build a dam.

The dam creates a pond where the beavers store more branches.

In the winter the branches stay fresh in the icy pond, providing food for the beavers.

In the rainforest

Rainforests are hot, steamy places, where rain falls almost every day. The world's biggest rainforest grows around the Amazon River in South America. Here are some animals that live there.

Macaw (a kind of parrot)

Sloths spend their lives hanging from branches.

This colourful **morpho butterfly** measures 11cm across its wings.

These leaf-cutting **ants** are everywhere on the forest floor.

Howler monkeys get their name because they screech loudly.

Hummingbirds flap their wings between 50 and 80 times a second. This makes a loud humming noise.

The **anaconda** is the world's heaviest snake.

Getting around

Some monkeys have tails that they can curl round branches and use to grip on tightly.

Tree frogs have sticky pads on their toes for climbing trees.

On safari

In parts of Africa there are huge grassy plains called 'savannah'. Many animals graze or hunt there.

The African **elephant** is the world's largest land animal.

Herds of **zebra** feed on the grass.

Wildebeest

Lions live in a family group called a pride.

Gazelle

Fun Fact

You can tell African and Indian elephants apart by their ears. African ears are bigger.

Scavengers

Hyenas are scavengers. They hang around to c up any food left over from kills made by bigger animals.

Vultures circle in the air until they see a dead animal on the ground. They must wait their turn to feed after the lions and hyenas.

Giraffe

The **cheetah** is the world's fastest animal. It can run at 80km/hr.

Baboon

In the outback

Many unusual animals are found only in Australia.

The call of the **kookaburra** bird sounds just like someone laughing.

The **emu** bird cannot fly but it can run fast.

Kangaroos graze in groups. They hop on their strong back legs.

The **duck-billed platypus** swims underwater to find its food.

Pouch baby

A newborn kangaroo is only about 2.5cm long. It lives inside its mother's pouch until it is big enough to leave.

Koala bears live in eucalyptus trees. They eat the leaves.

The **wombat** burrows amongst trees and rocks looking for plants to eat.

A baby kangaroo is called a **joey**.

Animals with pouches for their babies are called **marsupials**.

Under the ocean

Beneath the surface of the oceans there are many millions of animals of different shapes and sizes.

Hammerhead shark

Sea cows float along eating ocean plants.

Manta rays may grow up to 7 metres wide.

Some **seasnakes** are very poisonous.

Sea anemones use their tentacles to catch small creatures to eat.

Sea cucumber

Starfish

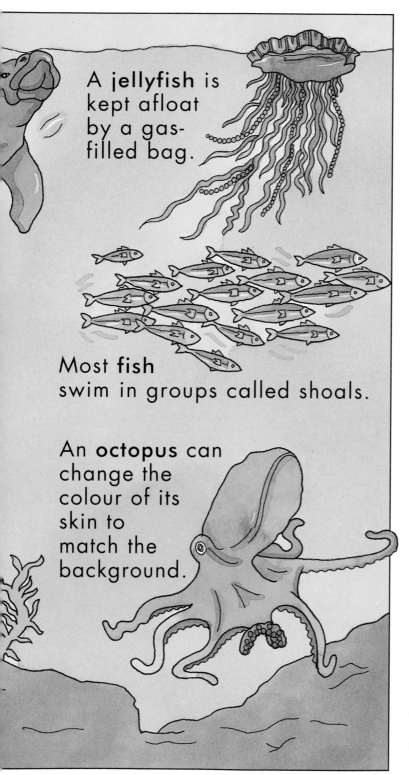

A **jellyfish** is kept afloat by a gas-filled bag.

Most **fish** swim in groups called shoals.

An **octopus** can change the colour of its skin to match the background.

Deep down

At the bottom of the ocean it is very dark and cold. The few animals that live there are strange and fierce-looking.

Deepsea fish often have big gaping mouths and long fangs.

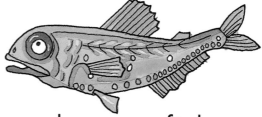

Some deepsea fish have spots of light on their skin to attract prey.

On the mountainside

High up on mountainsides it is often cold and rocky. Only a few types of animals live there.

These yaks have thick, warm coats. They live in the Himalayas.

Mountain goats can climb and jump very well. This type is called an **ibex**.

Mountain lions normally hunt alone at night.

Andean condor

Some mountain birds have large wings that are good for soaring on the wind.

Giant pandas are very shy and difficult to spot. They live in China.

Sleeping through

Some small mountain animals **hibernate**. They sleep through the cold winter.

Alpine marmots

They often sleep in cosy burrows underground.

When spring arrives they come outside to feed.

Some wild animals live in towns and cities. They usually come out at night when it is quiet to scavenge for food in wastebins and refuse tips.

Stray cat

Bat

Birds sometimes nest under roofs and in chimney pots.

Brown rat

Fox (Europe), coyote (North America) or wild dog (Asia, Africa)

Lizard (in warm countries)

Black rat

Insects, such as cockroaches

Mouse

Surprise visitors

Bears sometimes raid town dustbins in North America.

Elephants sometimes scavenge for food in parts of India.

Animals in danger

These animals are all endangered. This means that there are very few left in the world so they could become extinct.

Siberian tiger (Asia)

Lemur (Madagascar)

Green turtle (Pacific Ocean)

Humpback whale

Hyacinthine macaw (Amazon rainforest)

Mountain gorilla (Central Africa)

Snow leopard (Asia)

Animal threats

In some parts of the world **forests** are being cut down, destroying many animal homes.

Pollution can poison animals. **Litter** can harm them.

Some animals are **hunted** for their fur or their horns.

Index

Edited by Nicola Wright and Dee Turner
Consultant; Andrew Woodward
Design Manager; Kate Buxton
Printed in China

ISBN 1 84238 660 X

10 9 8 7 6 5 4 3 2 1

This edition first published in 2003 by
Chrysalis Children's Books
The Chrysalis Building, Bramley Rd, London W10 6SP

Copyright © Chrysalis Books PLC